GLASNOST: THE GORBACHEV REVOLUTION

Elizabeth Roberts

Hamish Hamilton · London

PEOPLE AND ISSUES

HAMISH HAMILTON CHILDREN'S BOOKS

Published by the Penguin Group
27 Wrights Lane, London W8 5TZ, England
Viking Penguin Inc, 40 West 23rd Street, New York, New York 10010,
U.S.A.
Penguin Books Australia Ltd, Ringwood, Victoria, Australia
Penguin Books Canada Ltd, 2801 John Street, Markham, Ontario,
Canada L3R 1B4
Penguin Books (N.Z.) Ltd, 182–190 Wairau Road, Auckland 10, New
Zealand

Penguin Books Ltd, Registered Offices: Harmondsworth, Middlesex,
England

First published in Great Britain 1989 by
Hamish Hamilton Children's Books

L7.276/3947.085

British Library Cataloguing in Publication Data
CIP data for this book is available from the British Library

ISBN 0–241–12653–3

The author and publisher would like to credit the following sources:

Dev Murarka, *Gorbachov, The Limits of Power*, Hutchinson 1988
S. V. Utechin, *Russian Political Thought*, J. M. Dent & Sons 1963
E. Lampert, *Sons Against Fathers*, Oxford University Press 1965
Mikhail Gorbachev, *Perestroika*, Collins 1987
B. H. Sumner, *Survey of Russian History*, Methuen & Co. Ltd 1961
Alexander Yakovlev (Ed.), *Perestroika Annual*, Futura 1988

Thanks also to the Great Britain–USSR Association for invaluable
assistance and advice.

Printed in Great Britain by
Butler and Tanner Ltd, Frome, Somerset

CONTENTS

Mikhail Gorbachev, who was elected to lead the Soviet Union in 1985.

1
INTRODUCTION

Glasnost is the name of a new policy introduced in the Soviet Union by Mikhail Gorbachev. Glasnost* means openness – in other words, talking frankly about all kinds of problems in Soviet society. In the 1980s, these problems included excessive government bureaucracy combined with corruption, poor public health care, alcoholism, inadequate housing, shortages in the shops and a stagnant economy. It cost the State more to provide essential goods and services, like food and rent, than the fixed low prices paid by the consumer. Also, Soviet currency (the rouble) could not be used outside the borders of the Soviet Union which made international trade difficult. On a different level, the country's intellectual and creative life had been stifled and Russian history was subjected to heavy censorship. Soviet people had been denied access to the so-called 'blank pages' of the Soviet past.

Mikhail Gorbachev was elected General Secretary of the Communist* Party of the Soviet Union in 1985. The Communist Party is the only party allowed in the Soviet Union at present, and it is run by a group called 'the Politburo'*. The General Secretary of this group of up to thirty members is the head of the Soviet government. Gorbachev was 54 years old – by far the youngest leader since the early Communist leaders, Vladimir Ilyich Lenin

*See glossary

The old guard: (*front row, far left*) Alexei Gromyko; (*third from left*) Konstantin Chernenko; (*centre*) Leonid Brezhnev; (*far right*) Yuri Andropov.

(in office 1917–1922) and Joseph Stalin (in office 1929–1953). At the time, little was known about the processes within the hierarchy of the Party leadership which led to his election, although later some details came out. He succeeded three old men who had died one after the other within three years of each other. The first, Leonid Brezhnev, had been the leader of the Soviet Union for 18 years. He died in 1982. The next head of government was Yuri Andropov who survived mostly as a bedridden invalid for two years before dying in 1984, followed by Konstantin Chernenko who tottered on for only one year as General Secretary before he too succumbed. Mikhail

Gorbachev went on to be elected President, the official Head of the Soviet State (as distinct from the head of the government), at the age of 57 in 1988.

Gorbachev became the leader of an enormous empire which had been cruelly but not inaptly described as 'Upper Volta* with missiles' – that is, a country with third-world standards of living but superpower military status. His vast responsibilities encompassed a nation of 286 million people of many different nationalities, races and languages covering one sixth of the earth's surface. Under Brezhnev, who was in power between 1964–1982, the country had sunk into an uneasy slumber and stagnation. Everywhere there was corruption, both large and small scale, often resulting from the way the economy worked. Alcoholism was a threat to the whole life of the nation. Many drank very heavily, making home life a misery. Babies were born handicapped as a result and for this and other reasons, infant mortality had actually begun to rise (a unique phenomenon in an industrialised economy). The drink problem was in part historical and cultural – Russians have always had a tradition of heavy vodka drinking. It was considered unmanly to drink wine, although beer was a respectable 'chaser' for the hard stuff, vodka. But there was a greater underlying social, or even psychological reason. People were drinking to blur their perception of a life which had so little to offer. There were no incentives to do better or work harder, because wages were fixed at a very low rate. The Soviet joke: 'We pretend to work and they pretend to pay us' seemed particularly apt. There were very few tempting consumer goods available in the shops, such as videos or personal stereos, fashionable clothes or microwave cookers. Even cars were extremely expensive and in short supply. Access to foreign newspapers, magazines and books was available only to a privileged circle, which included high-ranking Party members, and certain government employees or workers in research institutes. Travel was limited within the Soviet Union and foreign travel was virtually impossible unless you were a highly placed bureaucrat. Families were never allowed to travel abroad together, for fear presumably – however unjustified – that they would not return. On the occasions when one member was allowed out with another, say a husband and wife without their children, the couple would have to go through vetting procedures by a committee of their local Party to check that they knew the 'right' answers to various questions that might be asked of them in the West.

There was unquenchable curiosity in the Soviet Union

about life outside its borders, but little way of satisfying it other than by reading carefully edited articles in magazines and by watching the occasional TV news report which emphasised aspects of Western life such as strikes, homelessness and unemployment. The Soviet government's policy of censoring and falsifying its own history and culture, led to a stultifying diet of public lies, 'official art' and approved literature. People became accustomed to accepting a dual version of reality: what they knew to be true from their own experience, and discussed in private between themselves, and what was written or said officially. Many national monuments, churches and other buildings were left to crumble away, neglected and forgotten. The environment was also suffering from acts of industrial vandalism and pollution. The wildlife living in Lake Baikal, once the largest area of pure water in the world, was dying from untreated effluent being poured out from factories onto its banks. The Aral Sea was being drained practically dry to water the cotton crops of Uzbekistan, creating a vast salt desert around the sea. The resulting contamination of the environment has caused birth defects and premature deaths in the local population.

Underlying all was the horrible knowledge never publicly admitted or discussed, that only a generation before, the whole country had been subjected to unimaginable terror. It is now believed that Joseph Stalin caused the death of no fewer than 40 million of his own countrymen and women during his long and awful reign.

Inefficiency due to clumsy and remote central government planning and irresponsible management, combined with human operator error, led to many accidents and at least one major nuclear disaster in the 1950s which

1 ESTONIA
2 LATVIA
3 LITHUANIA
4 MOLDAVIA
5 GEORGIA
6 AZERBAIJAN
7 ARMENIA

affected hundreds of kilometres of territory and thousands of people. But neither this, nor other tragedies, like air crashes or train collisions were ever discussed in the press. Finally, just over a year after Gorbachev came to power, the statistically inevitable result of these years of official cover-ups, muddle and mismanagement occurred: at 1.23 am on Saturday 26 April 1986 the number 4 reactor at the Chernobyl atomic power station in the Ukraine, 150 kilometres from the republic's capital

of Kiev, exploded. Initially officials at Chernobyl delayed notifying both the population of the surrounding countryside and central government in Moscow of the enormity of the disaster. It was an environmental monitoring station in Sweden which first alerted neighbouring countries in Europe that a radioactive cloud was drifting across their borders, depositing radio-active substances with the rain. When two leading members of the Politburo eventually went to Chernobyl to investigate the crisis two days after the accident, they were appalled to find that the true scale of the disaster had been kept from the leadership, and therefore, from the world.

The need for glasnost in Soviet life could no longer be said to be a matter of internal policy only. In the nuclear age, there are no national boundaries. 'We need glasnost as we need the air,' said Gorbachev in his book *Perestroika**, published in 1987 – a year after Chernobyl. How he achieved it is as exciting a story with as many twists, turns, setbacks and triumphs as any thriller.

2

THE BACKGROUND

Why had the Soviet Union fallen so far behind the developed world in so many aspects of everyday life? It was not for want of natural resources, whether measured in mineral wealth, rich earth for crops or the stamina of the Soviet people. The Soviet Union had suffered terribly in World War II – but then, so had other countries, Germany in particular. Even though Germany is a much smaller country than the Soviet Union (with fewer resources), by 1988 the standard of living of West Germans was among the highest in the world.

To understand the plight the Soviet Union found itself in, and the origins of authoritarian undemocratic government in Russia, it is necessary to look at some crucial aspects of Russian history. In the 9th and 10th centuries, small settlements developed in southern Russia (called 'Rus'), not unlike the city-states in Ancient Greece. In these city-states there were two authorities, a prince who represented military power and an assembly of free citizens, including merchants and farmers, called the 'veche'. They decided questions such as the election of mayors and sometimes acted like a supreme court to decide legal cases.

Over the next four centuries, one princely clan, the Rurik dynasty, established domination over the others, ruling first from Kiev and then, later, from Moscow. In 988, while the Rurik dynasty was still based in Kiev, the

Rurik prince, Vladimir, installed Orthodox Christianity as the official state religion. The story goes that he sent messengers to investigate the comparative merits of Judaism, Christianity and Islam. He ruled out Islam because of its prohibition of the consumption of alcohol: Prince Vladimir is said to have claimed, 'It is Russia's joy to drink, we cannot do without it'. The delegates who had gone to Constantinople (now Istanbul) to attend the Orthodox services in the great Cathedral of St. Sophia reported that 'they had not known whether they were on the earth or in heaven', it was so beautiful.

The establishment of Orthodox Christianity as the State religion was a major factor in shaping Russia's political development. This is because in this branch of Christianity, the Church concerns itself with the Life Everlasting and the eternal soul. It does not claim to have any say in non-religious matters and this attitude has prevented it from playing an active role in political affairs. In other European countries, and especially during the Reformation* in the 16th century, there have been fierce debates between Church and State, and the Church has often emerged as a stern critic of government excesses and helped to establish the rights and responsibilities of the individual. This is a role the Russian Church has never played.

The next landmark in Russian history was the so-called 'Tatar yoke'. From 1238 to 1480, Russia had to pay taxes to the fierce nomadic Tatar army initially led by Genghis Khan. The Tatars were Mongolians who conquered much of eastern and central Europe from their base in Asia. Part of their great success in horseback battle was a result of their invention of the stirrup. Curiously, this period gave the Russian Orthodox Church its first opportunity to demonstrate a willingness

A diorama showing a Mongol attack on Vladimir in 1238.

to co-operate with a pagan secular power (this was to be repeated in its relations with the Communist government 700 years later). On at least one occasion, for instance, the Church threatened to excommunicate all the inhabitants of the town of Novgorod for refusing to pay the Tatar taxes.

Russia emerged from the 'Tatar yoke' during the reign of Ivan III of Muscovy (1462–1505), the first ruler of Russia to call himself Tsar of all Russia. (Tsar comes from 'Caesar', the title given to the rulers of the Roman Empire.) Ivan III, also known as 'the Great', ran the country according to the following principles, which were to set a pattern for the future:

1 The Tsar embodied divine authority to rule with unlimited power.
2 All the Tsar's subjects owed service to the State, of which he was the semi-sacred embodiment.
3 The subjects included the landed gentry, who were obliged as a result to serve the Tsar either in the army or as administrators.
4 The State was all-powerful because it was identified with the Tsar.
5 No clearly independent institutions developed, for instance: a parliament to make laws and judges to apply them. Both these jobs were just part of a centralised bureaucracy which grew on an exceptionally large scale.
6 The military needs of the State were considered the most vital, which made the army the first concern of Tsarism and intensified the use of force and police action in government.

Another important aspect of Tsarist Russia was the introduction of serfdom. Between 1480–1700 the condition of serfdom enslaved the majority of the population. The peasants became serfs which meant that they were tied to their landlords and obliged to work for them in return for living on their land. The idea of serfdom was elaborated and laws were passed to regulate the way it worked but without it becoming feudalism*. In other parts of Europe, feudalism entailed the idea of a personal bond between master and man, in which the master had an obligation to protect his vassals (workers) in return for their labour.

Removal* of whole populations first occurred in the

The tyranny of tsarism was embodied in Ivan IV, who became known as 'the Terrible'.

reign of Ivan III when Ivan succeeded in making Novgorod part of his new Russian state. 'Novgorod the Great' had been a rival trading centre and city-state which blocked Ivan III's access to the Baltic sea trading routes. ('Removal' was last practised by Stalin on the Crimean Tatars and others in the 1940s, in revenge for their allegedly lending support to Hitler's invading German army.)

Tsar Ivan the Terrible (reigned 1533–1584) is remembered as the cruellest Tsar in Russian history. Although his reign was bloody, he consolidated Russia's territory by defeating her enemies abroad and tightened the grip of central government at home.

The next notable Tsar after Ivan the Terrible was Peter the Great. 'The impact of Peter the Great (born 1672, reigned 1689–1725) was like that of a peasant hitting his horse with his fist' (B. H. Sumner, *Survey of Russian History*). Peter the Great tinkered in various ways with the internal structure of the government – he re-organised the nobility, for instance, into a 'Table of Ranks' which put everyone once and for all in their place. The Table laid down fourteen ranks or 'chiny' in the army and navy, and fourteen in court or civilian spheres. It was possible to acquire hereditary titles of nobility in certain ranks. The Table of Ranks also set out details such as how many horses and the sort of carriage a member could run, and what sort of finery he could wear. The wearing of lace, for instance, was restricted to the top five ranks of the 'chiny'. Peter the Great also strengthened the bureaucracy and invented the 'senate' – a sort of ministry of ministers to act during his many absences on foreign wars.

Internal passports were one of his less happy inventions, and to this day Soviet citizens are not free to settle wherever they please inside their own country. But Peter's reign marked a surge of interest in foreign technology and 'know-how'. Peter himself stayed in Holland and in Deptford near the river Thames in London to learn about shipbuilding. He also sent young Russians abroad specifically to learn from the West. As a result, a tension arose between those who believed that Russia had much to gain from increased contact with the West and those who believed that the West had nothing to offer except corruption of Russia's unique national character and institutions.

During the years which followed Peter the Great's reign, Russia consolidated her position as a European power, notably as a partner in the alliance with Britain, Austria and Prussia formed to defeat Napoleon. This led in turn to ordinary Russian troops and their officers getting a glimpse of Western capitals such as Paris after Napoleon's defeat in 1814. Thus, a generation of impressionable young noblemen got a firsthand taste of Western liberties and constitutional ideas which they began to try to introduce at home unsuccessfully during the following one hundred years. Nothing, it seemed, would achieve the reformers' aims but a total overthrow of the whole system and a new start.

One young nobleman who returned from serving with the army in Paris to stir up liberal opinion was Peter Chaadayev. In 1836 (during the reign of Nicholas I) he published an article which was to highlight a growing debate between those who wished to see Russia in the mainstream of European cultural and political development (the Westernisers) and those who sought the preservation of 'holy mother Russia' (the Slavophiles). Chaadayev claimed that Russia 'stood alone in the world' not belonging to East or West, and not having

The 'westernising' of Russia: Peter the Great ordered his men to cut short the traditional long overcoats worn by Russian nobles.

contributed 'a single idea to the mass of human ideas'.

Both the Westernisers and the Slavophiles were opposed to the autocratic regime of Nicholas I, but they had different aspirations for the future of Russia. The Westernisers wished to overturn the structure of society and approved of Peter the Great's policies as having represented 'radical change' in Russia. On the other hand, the Slavophiles looked to a return to a rather idealised view of the old ways of the pre-Peter period. They wished to retain the old structure with certain reforms. There are echoes of this debate today in the era of glasnost. Supporters of Gorbachev seek changes in the Soviet Union on a similar scale to Peter the Great's reforms, while the nationalist movement, Pamyat, believes in the Slavophile approach that Russia should look within its own culture and traditions for less radical solutions to problems. Pamyat is also tainted by anti-Semitism*, a relic of pre-Revolutionary Russia which is rejected by Gorbachev and his supporters.

Three Slavophile ideas in particular passed into later threads of Russian thought: the concept of 'sobornost' (the value of decisions made together on the basis of shared belief), the notion of the communal spirit of the Russian people and Pan-Slavism. Slavs are people who share a family of languages and racial origins in Eastern Europe, including Russians, Bulgarians, Serbo-Croats, and Poles. Pan-Slavism is the idea that all Slavs share certain valuable ethnic qualities and should therefore make common cause together as a cultural bloc. Slavophiles also promoted the idea that people should return to simple rural values.

By the 19th century, Tsarism had come to represent autocracy, Orthodoxy and Nationality. The 'Theory of Official Nationality' incorporated many of the Slavophile ideals. It was formulated by the political philosopher and some time Minister of Education S. S. Uvarov (1786–1855). It has been defined as: 'devotion to the Russian national heritage and the spiritual make-up of the people, a refusal to trust Western Europe as a model for Russia or West European theories as at all relevant for Russia; it also implied a concern for the interests and well-being of the people.' (S. V. Utechin, *Russian Political Thought* 1963).

In 1855 a new Tsar, Alexander II (reigned 1855–81) had come to power. He is known as the reforming Tsar, and various interesting comparisons can be drawn between his situation and Gorbachev's. Both men came to power at a time of low national morale in the face of military humiliation. In 1856 the Russian Empire was defeated in the Crimean War by Britain and France. At the beginning of the Gorbachev era many young Soviet soldiers had lost their lives in attempting to support an unpopular Communist regime in Afghanistan. Furthermore, Alexander II earned the title of the 'reforming Tsar' by agreeing to emancipate the serfs in 1861. This was a mixed blessing for the peasants, who thereby gained their 'liberty' but lost their right to live on the land. However, it was a bold gesture and the phrase 'revolution from above' was coined to describe this reform. Mikhail Gorbachev picked up this phrase and used it to describe his own initiatives in his book *Perestroika*.

Towards the end of the 19th century, there had developed a new class in Russian society, the intelligentsia. Indeed, the word was invented in Russian. These were educated people usually outside government circles and not always from the traditional 'ruling classes' who had the power to influence opinion through their writing. In

No. 128.

THE BELL.

APRIL 8, 1862.

REGISTERED AT THE GENERAL POST-OFFICE FOR TRANSMISSION BEYOND THE UNITED KINGDOM.

КОЛОКОЛЪ

VIVOS VOCO!

Выходитъ два раза въ мѣсяцъ въ Лондонѣ.
Цѣна 6 пенсовъ. Печатается въ Вольной
Русской Типографіи, 136 & 138 Caledonian
Road, N.

ЛИСТЪ 128.

8 Апрѣля 1862.

(WITH SUPPLEMENT No. 9.)

У Трюбнера & Co., въ книжной лавкѣ,
60, Paternoster Row, и у Тхоржевскаго,
1, Macclesfield Street, (Gerrard Street),
Soho, London. Price six-pence.

ФИНАНСОВАЯ РЕФОРМА ВЪ РОССІИ.

Отрывокъ изъ находящагося въ печати сочиненія :

"ESSAI SUR LA SITUATION RUSSE."

(Lettres à un anglais).

Реформа состояла въ централизаціи финансовыхъ учрежденій въ одинъ государственный банкъ.....

Заемный банкъ, сохранныя казны и приказы общественнаго призрѣнія въ сущности составляли одинъ родъ банковъ, которыхъ оборотъ заключался въ безотговорочномъ принятіи крупныхъ и мелкихъ вкладовъ за 4 сложныхъ процента, съ обязательствомъ возврата капиталовъ съ процентами по предъявленіи, и въ приложеніи вкладовъ преимущественно къ долгосрочному поземельному кредиту, т. е. въ употребленіи оныхъ на ссуды подъ залогъ недвижимыхъ населенныхъ имѣній, обычно на 37 лѣтъ по 6 или (5+1) % годовыхъ взносовъ. Одинъ лишній процентъ за ссуду противъ процентовъ платимыхъ по вкладамъ и единовременный 1 % премію при ссудѣ—шли на содержаніе воспитательныхъ домовъ и самыхъ кредитныхъ учрежденій и на покрытіе вѣроятностей немедленнаго востребованія доли вкладовъ. Эти кредитныя учрежденія можно уподобить англійскимъ joint-stock banks (банкамъ соединенныхъ вкладовъ), или еще вѣрнѣе—огромнымъ сберегательнымъ кассамъ (saving - banks), готовымъ принять и пустить въ обращеніе деньги, сбереженныя кладымъ, большія и малыя, безъ ограниченія суммы.

Новый "государственный банкъ" соединялъ въ себѣ : "Экспедицію кредитныхъ билетовъ, заемный банкъ, коммерческій банкъ и с. петербургскую сохранную казну;" остальные сберегательные банки (saving-banks) поступали подъ его вѣдѣніе, приводясь въ постепенную ликвидацію. Еще до основанія государственнаго банка, правительство, въ 1857 году, уменьшало проценты по вкладамъ съ 4 на 3 сложныхъ

процента ; а въ послѣдствіи на 2 % простыхъ и учреждало 4-хъ процентные и черезъ шесть мѣсяцевъ 5-ти процентные непрерывно-доходные банковые билеты (погашаемы въ 41 и 37 лѣтъ) для выкупа вкладовъ изъ сберегательныхъ банковъ. Съ учрежденіемъ государственнаго банка поземельный кредитъ былъ удержанъ (на 37 лѣтъ по 6 % годовыхъ взносовъ) до выплаты уже занятыхъ суммъ ; всякій-же дальнѣйшій поземельный кредитъ былъ прекращенъ. Коммерческій учетъ, бывшій долгомъ коммерческаго банка, долженъ былъ сдѣлаться одной изъ главныхъ операцій государственнаго банка. "Коммиссія погашенія государственнаго долга" осталась внѣ администраціи государственнаго банка, относясь къ нему банкъ равный къ равному, свыше руководимыя "совѣтомъ финансовыхъ учрежденій" подъ предсѣдательствомъ министра финансовъ. Управленіе государственнаго банка было поручено барону Штиглицу, который — вслѣдствіе неприязненныхъ отношеній къ министру и двору—закрылъ было свой собственный банкъ, первый торговый домъ и имперіи и одинъ изъ первыхъ въ Европѣ; но вскорѣ—когда лондонскій заемъ выполнить не удался—былъ обласканъ министромъ и дворомъ, заключилъ миръ, получилъ орденъ и посвятилъ себя благодействію Россіи.

Прежде чѣмъ я выскажу вамъ нѣкоторыя замѣтки о финансовой реформѣ, я поставлю вамъ на видъ хронологическій порядокъ кой-какихъ цифръ, взятыхъ съ оффиціальныхъ документовъ.

СОСТОЯНІЕ ГОСУДАРСТВЕННАГО ДОЛГА

въ 1856 г.[*]

Долговъ срочныхъ внѣшнихъ, голландскими гульденами	53,448,000
Долговъ внутреннихъ срочныхъ, сер. рублей	145,338,045
Долговъ безсрочныхъ (внѣшнихъ и внутреннихъ), с. рублей	267,990,012
Долговъ безсрочныхъ (по займу для окончанія Спб. - моск. дороги) фунтовъ стерл.	5,060,000[†]
Всего на серебро рублей	476,615,039

[*] Къ 1 Января, слѣдственно цифры относятся къ истекшему году.

[†] Я беру цифры какъ онѣ показаны въ академическихъ мѣсяцесловахъ и въ отчетахъ министра финансовъ.

* Кромѣ поземельнаго кредита, сохранныя казны производили ссуды подъ залогъ движимыхъ имуществъ, ссуды сравнительно съ поземельнымъ кредитомъ чрезвычайно незначительныя (въ отношеніи къ поземельному кредиту былъ 1 къ 117). Причина такой ничтожности движимаго кредита, конечно, заключалась въ ограниченіи ссуды только для двухъ сложныхъ ; но я'мъ также и не намѣкать въ этомъ фактѣ государствующей потребности поземельнаго кредита въ странѣ преимущественно земледѣльческой.

Годъ VI.

The Bell: this radical émigré periodical was published in London to avoid official Russian censorship in the 19th century. Its editor, Alexander Herzen, was a founding father of the intelligentsia.

the absence of an official opposition within the government and in the face of censorship the intelligentsia took on the role of the conscience of the nation. Today, it is through the intelligentsia that Gorbachev is trying to promote his reforms ('perestroika') using the policy of glasnost. It was members of the intelligentsia who were to lead the revolutionary movements which culminated in the overthrow of the Tsarist government in 1917.

3
THE CONVERSION TO COMMUNISM

At the turn of the century, there were tensions within Russian society arising from the reluctance of Tsar Nicholas II (acceded 1894) to embark firmly on a course of social reform which might have led to the successful development of parliamentary democracy and a monarchy limited by a constitution. The emancipation of

Tsar Nicholas II with his family.

the serfs had led peasants to ask why so much land remained in the possession of so few people. Some peasants had prospered, leaving the majority worse off than before. The population had grown, and although towns and industrial jobs were on the increase, most of the extra mouths to feed were in rural areas because there were restrictions on mobility of labour. A series of famines caused severe suffering. In 1905, a revolution occurred. A wave of strikes and demonstrations, some led by professional revolutionaries (including Leon Trotsky and Lenin), others spontaneous expressions of long pent-up frustration, followed a disastrous war with Japan. Police fired on a crowd which was trying to deliver a petition to the Tsar. In the aftermath, the Tsar agreed to a charter setting out five civil liberties, which included freedom of speech and association. A representative assembly was to share the making of laws with the Tsar. However, there were no guarantees that the Tsar would keep to the agreement, and many conservative advisers were against the idea of parliamentary democracy.

Social tensions were savagely intensified by the disaster of World War I (1914–18). The course of the war went very badly for the Russian army, ill-equipped and poorly led. These tensions came to a climax in the Revolution of 1917 which led to the overthrow of the Tsar.

The Russian Revolution of 1917 had two phases: February and October. In February, the Tsar was overthrown and a provisional government set up. Meanwhile, people's committees (soviets) were being elected in an attempt to establish a new source of power by more radical political factions in factories and other meeting places. Some regiments in the army had mutinied. After several months of discussions and uncertainty, while power swung between the liberals on the one hand and

The Communists storm the Winter Palace, seat of the government, in 1917. This picture is a scene from the Eisenstein film *October*.

the Communists (Bolsheviks) on the other, matters were brought to a head. The Communists were the only party to promise land reform – the one thing the Russian peasantry most longed for and understood: the right to occupy and cultivate their own plots of land. In October, Trotsky, by now a leading Communist, took power in the then capital St. Petersburg, which had been renamed

'Petrograd' because of the war with the Germans ('burg' is a word of German origin meaning town and 'grad' is the old Russian word for town). The Prime Minister of the Provisional government, A. F. Kerensky, fled, and most other ministers were arrested. Lenin, who had been in hiding since July 1917, emerged to greet the dawn of a new era. An election was held in November 1917 for a Constituent assembly made up of different political factions, including the socialists and liberals, in which the Communists won only a quarter of the votes. Therefore, when the assembly met in January 1918, Lenin and the Communists, impatient to gain power, decided to dissolve it by force, with the help of sections of the army sympathetic to their cause.

The Communists took power with these immediate aims: to negotiate peace terms with the Germans, give the land to the peasants, establish complete workers' control of the factories and release all stocks of food to relieve the famine then afflicting many parts of Russia. In the longer term, it was their declared aim to spread their revolution throughout the world. This overall goal was based on the philosophy of Karl Marx. Marx was a 19th century German economist and philosopher who believed that society should be based on equality and that everything should be communally owned. He predicted that the poor industrial urban workers of the world, the 'proletariat', would rise up against the owners of capital (capitalists) and seize power. Lenin, Trotsky and others developed a practical political system, called Communism, based on a combination of Marx and Lenin's theories.

The October Revolution of 1917 was intended to transform society. The old system, where the Tsar was absolute ruler, was swept away. The Tsar and his family were murdered in July 1918. At the time, few people would have thought that the new Communist system could ever have anything in common with the old. But

Lenin addressing a meeting in Moscow. The figure in semi-uniform on the right is Trotsky.

many bad aspects of the old society, such as lack of personal and political freedom, restrictions on freedom of speech, an ever-watchful secret police and the dead weight of a great state bureaucracy, remained. Oddly enough, as the Soviet system of government evolved it came to resemble in many negative respects the autocracy it had replaced in 1917.

Lenin was the first leader of the Communist Party after the Revolution. Decrees were passed which were eventually to provide free education for all, a national insurance system, health care, pensions and other benefits hitherto unheard of in any other country in the world. But the early years of the Communist regime in what became known as the Union of Soviet Socialist Republics took a terrible toll. A civil war followed the Revolution, and a syndicate of Western nations invaded the Soviet Union in a half-hearted attempt to bolster Russian support for the war effort against Germany, and to assist the White Army, opposed to the Bolshevik, or Red Army. In order that his government should survive, Lenin introduced various extreme measures which were to become known as 'War Communism'. Food and other supplies were rationed and surplus grain had to be sold to the government at fixed prices. Anyone caught trading in any goods other than through State shops was liable to be shot on sight. It was under Lenin, too, that the policy of eliminating successful peasant farmers (called 'kulaks') began. This was justified as an attempt to remove middle-class elements entirely from Soviet society. Also, at this time concentration camps were set up to isolate potential opponents of the system. For seventy years none of this could be discussed in the Soviet Union, where Lenin's reputation was as sacred as the Tsar's once had been. Only in 1988 could it be broached for the first time, as the floodgates opened under Gorbachev's new policy of glasnost.

By 1921 the period of 'War Communism' was over, and Lenin introduced economic reforms in an attempt to revive the supplies of goods in the shops. This was called the New Economic Policy or NEP for short. NEP allowed some free enterprise, that is, people were allowed to open small shops or restaurants and peasants were allowed to trade privately in grain. This short-lived experiment in individual enterprise was discontinued a few years after Lenin died in 1924, but one of Gorbachev's new policies is to encourage small businesses again. Lenin's successor, Joseph Stalin, was meanwhile to prove a worse tyrant than any Tsar, wielding total power from the Kremlin* (seat of the central government) for over thirty years.

Stalin decided that everything was to be sacrificed in order to make the Soviet Union an industrialised power. Agriculture was to be entirely nationalised, and he ordered that the whole class of wealthy peasants (kulaks) was therefore to be eliminated, and their lands confiscated.

Soviet historians now admit that the majority of these so-called 'kulaks' were in fact merely peasants who had been granted land at the time of the Revolution, and their crime was simply to practise good husbandry. As a result, the original supporters of the 1917 Revolution were penalised for their hard work. Farms were collectivised* (pooled) and run strictly according to Party orders, even down to the date for the sowing of seeds – regardless of local climatic conditions.

Soviet agriculture has never recovered from this policy. A country which used to export wheat to the rest of the world before World War I henceforth started to experience severe difficulties in feeding its own population. By

Stalin (pictured with Lenin on the wall) ruthlessly industrialised the USSR.

1932–33, food supplies from the countryside were requisitioned for the towns, and as a result millions of men, women and children starved to death in the Ukraine and other parts of the Soviet Union. Glasnost still has to reveal the full details of this horrifying policy which was deliberately undertaken to crush any resistance to Stalin's total control of the economy. The power of propaganda to deceive was shown most vividly at this time because, even when the famine was at its height, many Western observers wrote glowing recommendations of the Soviet system under Stalin.

One British journalist who saw through the propaganda was Malcolm Muggeridge, writing for the *Manchester Guardian* newspaper. It was difficult to send uncensored reports from the USSR back to Britain, but Muggeridge occasionally managed to avoid the censor's pen by sending his reports via British diplomatic sources. In 1933 he wrote, 'In both the Ukraine and the North Caucasus the grain collection has been carried out with such thoroughness and brutality that the peasants are now quite without bread ...'

Other visitors to the Soviet Union, like the British socialists Beatrice and Sidney Webb, and the writer Bernard Shaw were apparently taken in by the official deception. Bernard Shaw wrote after a trip to Russia that he 'did not see a single under-nourished person in Russia, young or old'. The Webbs placed the blame for some food shortages on 'a refusal of the agriculturalists to sow.... or to gather up the wheat when it was cut'.

Up to the very dawn of glasnost there have been many Westerners from all walks of life who have visited the Soviet Union and chosen to see conditions of life there not as they were (and are) but in the idealised form that their official hosts presented to them.

Stalin's policies caused millions to starve to death in the countryside.

In the 1930s Stalin also initiated large-scale 'purges' of the founding members of the Communist government and of old Communist Party members in rigged show trials where the 'guilty men' were paraded and forced to make 'confessions' after being tortured. Stalin accused them of plotting to assassinate him and other Stalinist party leaders, with the aim of overthrowing the Soviet regime and re-establishing capitalism in the Soviet Union. These people's reputations are now being restored in articles in the Soviet press. Many millions of lesser victims of the Stalin terror, however, cannot be individually mentioned, but there is to be a monument to them in Moscow. (Trotsky, Stalin's most feared opponent, was sentenced to death in his absence, having fled abroad.

The execution was carried out when he was assassinated in Mexico in 1940.)

Just before World War II, in 1937, Stalin also decided that the Soviet army was plotting against him and most of the highest ranking generals and officers were arrested and shot. An atmosphere of fear, where even schoolchildren were encouraged to betray each other and their own parents, pervaded the whole country.

Terrible hardships and colossal civilian and military casualties were suffered by the Russian people during World War II (1939–45). In Russia, this war is known as the 'Great Patriotic War'. Russia only entered the war in 1941, when Germany invaded her. This act of aggression was a surprise, because Stalin had signed a secret pact with Hitler. Once the Soviets had joined in the war, they played a major part in the defeat of fascism* by the Allies. After the war was won, however, the reign of domestic terror continued until Stalin's death in 1953.

When the policy of glasnost was first announced officially by Gorbachev in 1985, the crimes of Stalin could not be fully and openly discussed in any Soviet media. It was known by word of mouth or from documents smuggled into the USSR that First Secretary* Nikita Khrushchev had denounced Stalin's reign of terror at a closed meeting of the Communist Party in the early hours of 25 February 1956. Copies of his speech were circulated through the country to be read out to the Party apparatchiks (officials) and then subsequently destroyed. The speech was finally published in the Soviet Union for the first time in April 1989.

DE-STALINISATION

> ❛ You cannot understand us or our actions unless you know our history. ❜
> Mikhail Gorbachev, December 1987

Soviet newspapers and magazines carry regular articles and letters from readers about the Stalin terror. The newly-formed anti-Stalinist 'Memorial' society exists to build monuments to the millions of Stalin's victims and to create a network of museums and historical research organisations to examine the Stalin phenomenon. It has also called for a posthumous public trial of Stalin. One of the most agonising features of the terror was that children, even tiny babies, were taken from their parents when they were arrested, given different names and brought up in children's homes. Conditions in these children's homes were like prison. The children were kept hungry – they were also being punished for their parents' 'crimes'. The Soviet historian Roy Medvedev estimates the number of Stalin's victims from 1927–53 at no fewer than 40 million. 'We are bound by our conscience,' he writes, 'to bring back those who didn't manage to come back on their own. To open the eyes, the heart, and to remember.'

Soviet author Anatoly Rybakov wrote in 1988: 'Thousands of victims of Stalin's repressions are still alive – the old, the sick, people without anything, living in dire straits. Millions of their children who bore the stigma "sons (daughters) of an enemy of the people" are also still alive, and other people whose fate is crippled and to whom the country owes an irredeemable debt. The names of the millions who were shot or who died in prison camps have not yet been given, their graves have not been found nor have monuments been put up . . .'.

The first of December is proposed as Memory Day for the victims of Stalin. It was on this day in 1934 that Stalin's nearest political rival for supreme power in the Soviet Union, Sergei Kirov, was assassinated – it is widely believed, on Stalin's orders.

The journalist Leonid Radzhikovsky wrote in *Moscow News* in November 1988, '1 December means ditches filled with skeletons, like those near Minsk; it means Norilsk, Magadan, Potma, Karaganda and the names of dozens of other cities which became the names of prisons. After 1 December [1934], millions of people would lie with open eyes and listen to the noise of the lift, of steps on the staircase – night after night, 365 nights a year . . . The finest peasants, intellectuals and Communists were killed, broken or corrupted, and with them – the finest human qualities in our social awareness. Mercy and dignity became a hindrance to survival. A civic stand, a critical, rational attitude to political developments meant definite destruction.'

4
GORBACHEV – THE SCENE IS SET

Mikhail Gorbachev is the man who was destined to attempt to introduce the rule of law and democracy to the Soviet Union at last. He was born the son of peasants at Privolnoye, a village in the Stavropol region on 2 March 1931. His parents Maria and Sergei had joined the newly established collective farm – Sergei was an agricultural machine operator – and they experienced the famine which followed collectivisation in the area. In 1935 Stavropol was renamed Voroshilovsk and the shadow of the Stalin terror fell on the region in 1937 when the whole local party committee was arrested and the secretary shot as an 'enemy of the people'. Then the war came, and when young Mikhail was aged 11 the Germans occupied Privolnoye for six months in the summer of 1942. Germans were told by their Nazi leaders that Russians were 'Untermensch' (subhuman) and the Germans behaved with great barbarity towards them, killing and looting. This, together with the experience of famine, must have created a great impression on young Mikhail's mind. He went back to school when the Germans retreated from Voroshilovsk which they had renamed Stavropol in 1943, and started to work part-time as a combine harvester operator in 1944, going to work full time in 1946 when he was 15 years of age. His family was desperately poor, and in a recent television documentary his mother Maria described how Mikhail missed his first term at

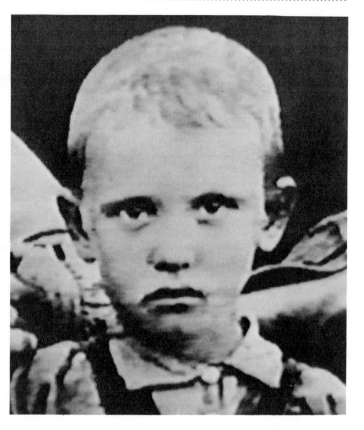

Young Mikhail, nicknamed 'Misha', grew up during the famine years.

school because he had no proper clothes and shoes to wear. His father wrote from the front to say that Mikhail must go to school, so she took their one sheep to market and sold it and bought a pair of good stout military boots for 1500 roubles – the equivalent of a month's wages. To get to school he had to walk 15 kilometres a day in all weathers, as well as having to catch up on all the work that he had missed through being absent for a term.

Moscow University, where Mikhail Gorbachev studied law and met his wife, Raisa.

In 1949 when he was 18, Mikhail Gorbachev received his first public recognition when he won the Order of the Red Banner of Labour. A year later, he went to Moscow University to study law, an appropriate subject for a future reformer. The curriculum in all Soviet university courses includes a unit in understanding the philosophy of Marxism-Leninism, the basis of Soviet Communism. The contrast between the theory and practice must have been striking, especially to a man with an analytical mind. A contemporary remembers that Gorbachev was particularly struck by the contrast between the theory of collective farm law and the reality. Gorbachev pointed out to his fellow students from personal experience that illustrations showing happy peasants sitting down to tables groaning with food were untrue. However, in 1952, at the age of 21, he joined the Communist Party. Like many of his generation, his best chance of changing things was from within the system. His first job in the Party was as an official of the Young Communist League*, a youth movement for 14–26 year-olds, and he travelled widely and spoke at meetings to encourage young people in the reconstruction of their country after the Nazi invasion.

In 1954 he married Raisa Titorenko, a fellow student from the Altai region in Siberia. Raisa was born in Rubtsovsk but grew up in Moscow. After university, Raisa became a lecturer and in 1956 she gave birth to their only daughter, Irina. At the time of Mikhail and Raisa's marriage, the death of Stalin and the appointment of Nikita Khrushchev as First Secretary ushered in a false dawn. The Khrushchev era was a time of great hope and promise, which was to be unfulfilled. There was a brief thaw in the strict censorship on all media imposed by Stalin, followed by a crackdown, and many of Khrushchev's over-ambitious pronouncements led in the end to nothing.

Amongst the worst mistakes of the Khrushchev era was his continued support of the geneticist Trofim Lysenko who first came to the fore in Stalinist Russia. Pre-war Soviet genetics (the study of genes) had been one aspect of its national science of which the country could be justly proud. However, Stalin had come to believe the claims of Lysenko, which were that plants or animals could pass on to their offspring characteristics acquired during their lifetime. For instance, plants enjoying ideal greenhouse conditions thrive and have abundant fruit. Lysenko believed that such plants' offspring would grow equally well wherever they were planted. In reality, plants and animals can only pass on certain improved qualities, such as cows which produce high yields of milk, through selective breeding to combine their genetic characteristics. Lysenko's theories set back progress in Soviet agriculture and medical research by many years. His mistaken ideas about the way plants can be improved meant that many years and millions of roubles were wasted planting unsuitable crops. For example, an attempt was made to grow maize, unsuccessfully, throughout the Soviet Union. Furthermore, it meant that during the Stalin and Khrushchev eras a whole generation of true geneticists were branded as enemies of the people for sticking to their scientific principles, and many died during the Stalin period in labour camps or prison.

Meanwhile, in 1955, the Gorbachevs had returned from university studies in Moscow to the Stavropol region where Mikhail's outstanding personal qualities, his straightforwardness, willingness to work hard, loyalty and intelligence marked him out for steady progress through the Party ranks. He had that quiet assurance that comes from having made his own way entirely in a world all too full of the privileged relations of Party bosses.

His first big break came when he was appointed First Secretary of the Young Communist League for the Stavropol region, with the specific task of improving agricultural production. He had backing from a senior official Fedor Kulakov, who helped him to get further promotions, and in due course Gorbachev was invited to Moscow, the centre of political power.

In 1961, Gorbachev attended the 22nd Congress of the Party as a delegate. At this congress Khrushchev announced a new and very ambitious party programme including de-Stalinisation, which reached its height the

Nikita Khrushchev: the extrovert who fell from power.

following year with the publication in the literary journal *Novy Mir* of Alexander Solzhenitsyn's account of life as a political prisoner in one of the Soviet labour camps: *One Day in the Life of Ivan Denisovich*. This gave a frank account of the hardships and injustices of Soviet society under Stalin, previously impossible to publish openly in an official journal.

However, Khrushchev's influence was beginning to wane because of general dissatisfaction with his haphazard initiatives at home and abroad. His promises of more freedom for artists and writers were proving to be inconsistent. When the great Russian writer Boris Pasternak, author of *Doctor Zhivago*, was awarded the Nobel Prize* for Literature, Khrushchev refused to let him leave the country to collect it. Khrushchev also encouraged officials of the Writers' Union to hound him to a premature death. They wrote and said terrible untrue things about him in public such as that he was an anti-Soviet agent, and expelled him from the Union. In 1962, Khrushchev managed to expose the world to a Soviet confrontation with the USA which threatened to lead to nuclear war, when he allowed missiles to be installed on Cuba. This became known as the Cuban missile crisis.

A final loss of confidence in Khrushchev's leadership occurred in October 1964, when leading members of the Politburo had the safe in Khrushchev's country house searched. They were said to have found there a list of the top people (including themselves) whom Khrushchev intended to replace at the forthcoming November session of the Central Committee*. (The Central Committee is a body of senior Communist officials who elect the Politburo and oversee the work of the ministries). Khrushchev was tricked into returning to Moscow and confronted with a blunt demand that he resign forthwith, to be replaced as First Secretary by one of his intended victims, Leonid Brezhnev. Another, Alexei Kosygin, became Prime Minister.

Today, Soviet commentators are beginning to re-examine the Khrushchev era in the light of Gorbachev's attempts at reform, opening yet another chapter of their recent history kept closed up till then, to try to learn from past mistakes. Many people believe that one day Khrushchev will be honoured in his homeland and abroad for his willingness to make contact with the West, as well as for dismantling the 'gulag' (prison system) set up by Lenin and Stalin.

The Brezhnev era is now known in the USSR as the period of 'zastoi' (stagnation) and, increasingly, as a period of corruption. For Gorbachev personally, it marked further improvement and success in his career. As First Secretary of the Stavropol District Party Committee he had the opportunity to experiment quietly with certain solutions to problems of agricultural method and organisation. He allowed the formation of teams of workers in each state farm who had both responsibility and a certain degree of freedom in achieving production targets. This contrasted with the usual practice, whereby the Chairman of the farm took all the decisions under the direction of the district Party bosses.

Under Gorbachev's leadership, agricultural production in the Stavropol district improved by 30–50%, whereas production in the rest of the country on the whole was doing badly. During this period of his life, Gorbachev was travelling increasingly, going abroad on delegations and sometimes even on holiday.

The Brezhnev era saw Soviet tanks roll into Czechoslovakia in 1968 to suppress reforms called 'socialism with a human face'.▶

As a matter of courtesy he had to call on a senior national Party official, Yuri Andropov, the head of the KGB* (secret police). Andropov spent his annual holiday in the Stavropol region and this formal duty grew into a friendship that was later to play an important part in Gorbachev's career.

Meanwhile, the Brezhnev era was gradually taking form. Brezhnev returned power firmly from central government to the 'cadres' (local Party bosses). At the time, this was promoted as a restoration of local democracy. However, with hindsight it can be seen to have been an open invitation to corruption and inertia on the part of officials who were more interested in having a quiet and comfortable life than setting about tackling deep-rooted problems in the country's economic management. Under Brezhnev, there was renewed pressure on the intelligentsia to toe the Party line. This conservatism was echoed in the Soviet Union's relations with its neighbours, particularly Czechoslovakia. In 1968, the First Secretary of the Czechoslovakian Communist Party, Alexander Dubček, launched a policy of reform that he called 'socialism with a human face' and became known as the 'Prague spring'. This was abruptly ended when Warsaw Pact* tanks, including Soviet tanks, rolled into the country to suppress the reforms and remove Dubček and his supporters forcibly from power. Dubček's policies were seen to be dangerous as they had transferred power from the hands of Communist Party officials into the hands of managers chosen for their skill rather than their political reliability.

Gradually, Soviet political life under Brezhnev became one of unscrupulous go-getting, all conducted under a gaudy canopy of meaningless medals, awards and prizes. Official Soviet accounts of life in the world outside were deliberately misleading: Soviet citizens were encouraged to believe that the capitalist West was on the verge of economic collapse whereas it was the countries of the Comecon* bloc (a trading union of mainly Eastern bloc countries) which were teetering on the edge of bankruptcy, suffering constant shortages and breakdowns of services. There is an old joke about the two leading Russian newspapers *Pravda* ('Truth') and *Izvestiya* ('The News'): 'There is no news in Truth and no truth in The News'. Never had this joke been more appropriate.

In his book *Gorbachov, the Limits of Power* the Indian journalist Dev Murarka described the situation thus: 'By the late 1970s the economic decline of the country became visible and dangerously distressing socially. A demoralised population was openly talking in terms of "razrukha" or devastation of the economy and society. Acute shortages of foodstuffs and consumer goods, hidden inflation, heavy drinking and corruption had become established as a normal part of life. This situation became all the more galling and humiliating as an expanding tourist flow to and from the Soviet Union brought home the disparity in living standards with the West and the contrast with the easy availability of consumer goods in most other parts of the world.'

Despite the worsening economic situation, and a stroke in 1976 which left him clinically dead for four minutes, Brezhnev and his entourage nevertheless continued to exert a strong grip on the reins of power. He had won the confidence of the military hierarchy, which previously had been alarmed by some of Khrushchev's wilder moves internationally (notably the Cuban missile crisis). Brezhnev had also the support of the political and bureaucratic hierarchy, who had enjoyed perks of office such as access to foreign luxury goods, special food shops and travel abroad under his benevolent protection. But he was a pathetic figure during his last years, literally led about like a shuffling performing bear by those who could not afford to let him retire.

The Brezhnev regime dragged on, but in the early 1980s it was shaken by a financial scandal which involved Brezhnev's daughter Galina with a diamond smuggling racket and other corruption cases near the top

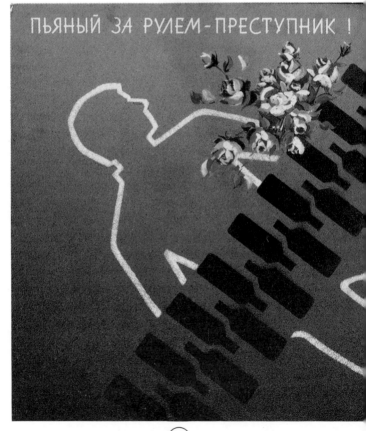

ПЬЯНЫЙ ЗА РУЛЕМ-ПРЕСТУПНИК !

of the hierarchy. (In 1988 her husband was put on trial for his life for economic crimes and was sentenced to 12 years imprisonment.) Finally, on 10 November 1982 Brezhnev died, and the stage was set for the succession struggle.

Brezhnev's successor as General Secretary of the Central Committee of the Communist Party was Yuri Andropov. At age 68, he won a narrow victory in the

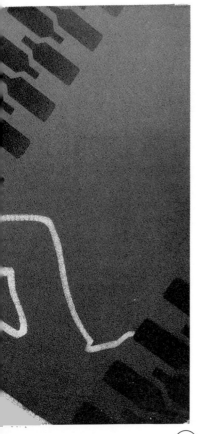

Yuri Andropov launched the campaign against alcoholism which was later to be taken up by Gorbachev. This poster says: BEING DRUNK AT THE WHEEL MAKES YOU A CRIMINAL.

election by the Politburo over another elderly candidate, Konstantin Chernenko, then aged seventy. Andropov, who had known Gorbachev since he was First Secretary of the Stavropol region, put Gorbachev in charge of various high-level duties, including the supervision of the cadres policy and leading an important delegation to Canada. Andropov started an energetic programme of social 'clean-up' aimed at corruption, drunkenness and indiscipline. However, he was very ill and within fifteen months he died. Before his death, he arranged for Gorbachev to be in line for succession. He obtained, with the help of the powerful Minister of Defence, Dmitri Ustinov, who had the confidence and backing of the Soviet Red Army, the formal agreement of Chernenko that Gorbachev should be his (Chernenko's) deputy.

Chernenko duly took over from Andropov in February 1984, but it was clear from the start that he was in very poor health, and 13 months later on 10 March 1985 he died. The way was clear for Gorbachev at last.

5
GLASNOST GETS INTO GEAR

Gorbachev was announced as the new General Secretary of the Central Committee of the Communist Party on 12 March 1985. Within six weeks he had strengthened his position by adding three of his supporters to the Politburo. Two weeks after that, his main rival for the post of General Secretary, Grigori Romanov, was removed from the Politburo. But these moves, although important, were not the most critical aspect of Gorbachev's first days in office. It was the new honesty and vigour which he displayed in his public appearances, most strikingly in a speech which he gave in May at the Smolny Institute in Leningrad. The Institute is intimately linked with the Revolution and Russian history, being Lenin's first headquarters in 1917. At Smolny, Gorbachev suggested in public for the first time that the Party itself had to take much of the blame for what had gone wrong, and implied that it either had to reform itself or face the consequences. The general public (of whom only 6% are invited to be members of the Party) were won over by this unheard-of candour. Gorbachev managed to combine a subtle sense of history with a frankness and personal appeal that had been totally lacking in the Soviet leadership since the days of Lenin himself. Previous leaders were rarely seen by the public and little was known about their family circumstances. It was not even generally known until

Gorbachev was the first modern Soviet leader to meet the public informally.▶

Andropov's funeral that he was married – his widow made her first and last public appearance when she came and wept by her husband's coffin but her name remained unknown to the public.

From the start, Gorbachev maintained physical contact with the people, talking to members of the general public or factory workers on televised 'walkabouts'. He also took Raisa with him on his visits round the country, and made it clear that she was a substantial partner not just a mute decoration. Raisa has taken a controversially active part as the Soviet Union's 'First Lady' since Gorbachev was elected General Secretary. Controversial, because no previous consort since Lenin's wife Krupskaya has been a public figure in the Soviet Union. There are still strong male chauvinist attitudes towards women in Russia. Also, she has clearly enjoyed the perks of status, such as possessing and using her American Express card in foreign luxury shops. At a time when the majority of Soviet women have little access to basics such as tights or cosmetics, her confident cosmopolitan appearance might seem tactless. However, she has played an important role in helping to change the image of the Soviet Union in the West.

Gorbachev had not only impressed the general public. He also caught the attention of a vital and powerful sector of influence: the Soviet intelligentsia. Gorbachev seemed to appreciate the importance both of listening to scientists, writers and other opinion-formers and of enlisting their support for the difficult changes that lay ahead. Stalin had imprisoned or shot a whole generation of these people, leaving the leadership of the Party without any effective opposition. Now the intellectuals began to hope that their views would be regularly taken into account by the leader of their country.

Raisa Gorbacheva: a new-style Soviet First Lady.

Change and renewal were the main themes of 'Perestroika' – the campaign started by Gorbachev to improve conditions in the Soviet Union. Perestroika and glasnost went together like a horse and carriage. Glasnost was the horse which drew perestroika. Perestroika means literally 'rebuilding' – in this context, perestroika means rebuilding Soviet society both physically and morally. Glasnost permits the public to take part in the analysis of what has gone wrong and needs to be put right. In his book *Perestroika*, Gorbachev says: 'I recall a meeting in June 1986 with the personnel of the apparatus of the . . . . . Central Committee. It concerned perestroika. I had to ask them to adopt a new style of working with the intelligentsia. It is time to stop ordering it about, since this is harmful and inadmissible. The intelligentsia has wholeheartedly welcomed the program for the democratic renewal of society.'

The first shots of the glasnost campaign were fired in the November 1985 issues of *Pravda* and *Izvestiya*. These were articles criticising local abuses of power by Party officials, and were backed up in later issues by letters from readers telling of their experiences at the hands of officious bureaucrats. In December Oleg Efremov, the Director of the Moscow Arts Theatre, staged a play called *Silver Wedding* in which the same theme was successfully treated. Also that December the Russian Republic Writers' Congress took up strongly the cause of the neglect of the national heritage and the mistreatment of the environment.

Widely respected writers in the Soviet Union called for second thoughts on a plan to reverse two great Siberian rivers in an irrigation project serving central Asia. In December 1985 themes were aired reminiscent of certain traditional Slavophile preoccupations; a dread that the unique character of 'Holy Mother' Russia was to be ruined by the debased Western 'PepsiCola / Rock and Pop' culture. Also that month the unpopular First Secretary of the Moscow City Party, Viktor Grishin, was replaced on Gorbachev's orders by Boris Yeltsin which was to prove a controversial appointment.

On 24 January 1986, Yeltsin launched an attack on what he called 'zones beyond criticism' within the Party organisation, in particular in Moscow itself. This bold step was followed in February by a major article in *Pravda* entitled 'Cleansing – a Frank Discussion'. The article consisted of a commentary linking many signed readers' letters which attacked abuses of power and privilege by Party officials, like access to special shops, hospitals and schools.

Boris Yeltsin set new standards of bold public criticism of the Party.

From their previous reputation as deadly dull supporters of the status quo, Soviet newspapers and magazines
suddenly became hot stuff. People who had used them in
the past as a necessary substitute for unobtainable toilet
paper now actually queued to read them. The boldest of
them all, such as *Moscow News*, were in great demand
and multiple 'wall newspapers' were built so that readers
who were unable to buy a copy could at least stand and
read the current issue in the street.

Crowds surround street displays of the outspoken weekly, *Moscow News*.

Glasnost served Gorbachev's purpose in the sense that issues like the need for realistic pricing and a shakeout of the labour force, involving redeployment and unemployment, could be broached in the press and therefore made familiar (if not acceptable) propositions for the public. One of his closest advisers, the sociologist Tatyana Zaslavskaya wrote in *Perestroika Annual*:

'. . . perestroika also brings certain disadvantages to the workers, which cannot be ignored: inevitable price increases for staple foodstuffs and services up to the level which will make their production and supply non-deficient and profitable; stepped-up rent rates for surplus housing over the State-guaranteed minimum; and so on. A potential cutting down of redundant jobs raises a spectrum of problems no less involved. This is the natural result of perestroika, the 'social price' which has to be paid for the acceleration of social and economic development in this country, for getting rid of our backwardness.'

The first major setback to the steady progress being made by Gorbachev on the home and international fronts was the explosion of the number 4 reactor in the nuclear power station at Chernobyl. This event had two crucial aspects, the disaster itself (and what it revealed about Soviet technology) and the way Gorbachev handled it. For the first time, his instinct for what was right and timely seemed to desert him. For days there was silence, other than from cryptic announcements by official spokesmen. Finally, Gorbachev himself appeared on Soviet television 18 days after the event and his speech was a rather strained and uneasy mixture of justification of Soviet delays in notifying their neighbours of the radiation cloud that was heading their way and an attack on the 'over-reaction' to the story by the Western press.

However, as life began to resume its normal course, so Gorbachev's policy of encouraging frankness and speaking out by writers, artists and film makers continued to bear fruit. In May, the distinguished writer and editor Vasily Bykov gave a press interview in which he explained the conditions in his home village in Byelorussia which had led up to some local people collaborating

After the explosion at Chernobyl, radioactive dust spread across Europe.

with the invading German army in 1941. He described the psychological wounds caused within a community by the cruel enforcement of collectivisation and the short-sightedness of the anti-religious campaigns in the early days after the Revolution. The effect of the campaign against the churches was to remove the moral force of a shared faith from the lives of the people. Misdeeds took place, such as unjust confiscation of goods and livestock, and the encouragement of children to denounce their own parents – acts which would have been condemned by religious leaders. Religion was seen as being connected with traditional values and the past. When it was mocked and banned, people felt that they had lost their history. Bykov pointed out that if people are told to despise the very institutions which have previously stood for the highest moral principles it can hardly be surprising if, as a result, they become confused and cynical about authority.

That same month of May 1986 saw the Cinematographers' Union Congress, the most significant so far in the processes of change sanctioned by Gorbachev. The Union members were all those who worked in the Soviet film industry, and the Union represented their interests, laying down conditions of work and pay. It also had links with the film industry overseas, organising conferences and delegations abroad. The members of the Union overthrew their old leaders who had presided over the gradual decline of Soviet cinema from a vital force in the country's intellectual life to a dog-eared remnant. They declared independence from censors and central funding, electing one of their most talented film makers, Elem Klimov, to head the Union.

In June the Congress of the Writers' Union took place. Just before the Congress opened, a group of leading writers and editors was invited to meet Gorbachev and he made it clear to them that he needed their help in fighting the forces of stagnation and corruption within the bureaucracy and the Party. This was an event of extraordinary significance, perhaps not fully understood even now. For the first time in Russian history, the leader of the country was calling on the intelligentsia to give him support of their free will. This is a historic partnership never before achieved in Russia, of the leader and the country's freest thinkers seeking to bring about change in the government and the bureaucracy. Gorbachev's tone was that of a moral and a political crusader, who saw that the economic health of the country could never be regained without cleaning up the double standards that pervaded Soviet life.

The Writers' Congress that followed this unprecedented meeting was predictably explosive, but failed to unseat the old guard to the same degree as had the Cinematographers' Union. A pervasive theme ran through the writers' speeches, a lament for lost culture, lost ethnic identity, a sense of being cheated of many great voices from the past either through suppression or censorship. Other themes emerged, too – the question of where responsibility for former mistakes must truly be laid, such as their treatment of Boris Pasternak. Some writers pointed out that it was wrong to single out individuals for brutal reprisals when to a certain extent all members of the Union bore some measure of blame.

An important occurrence in the literary scene at this time was the appointment of Vitaly Korotich as editor of the weekly magazine *Ogonyok*. Korotich was fairly typical of many members of the intelligentsia – as a young man in the 1960s he had the reputation of an outspoken poet in his native Ukraine. Then he had settled down to what seemed to be a rather conventional career as the editor of the Ukrainian magazine *Foreign Literature*, even writing for *Pravda* in the pre-glasnost days as a special correspondent toeing the anti-Western party line. However, under his editorship, *Ogonyok* has become one of the most outspoken champions of glasnost, leading the way with articles by and about the victims of Stalin, shortages and inefficiencies of the Soviet system, as well as publishing uncensored readers' letters and even – just before the extraordinary All-Union Party Conference in June 1988 – charging certain delegates with corruption.

The cumulative effect of the flood of revelations and recriminations in the Soviet press can be judged by the fact that by 1988 it had become necessary to cancel the final history examinations in every Soviet school because history itself was being rewritten! The official history text books were withdrawn, and a competition was announced for the best revised version, to contain the facts that now were being freely discussed as never before.

6

BACKLASH

By the autumn of 1988, Gorbachev had achieved much through his encouragement of free expression of opinion and criticism in nearly every area of Soviet life. Even bad conditions and low morale in the armed forces could be discussed in public. In international affairs, he had initiated the withdrawal of Soviet troops from Afghanistan and scored great personal triumphs at three 'Summit' conferences with the US President Ronald Reagan.

At home, he had steered his way through a complex conference – the special All-Union Party gathering for 5000 delegates and invited observers, held in Moscow in June 1988. This was a difficult occasion, because for the first time since he had been appointed to the leadership, there were strong signs that Gorbachev was being called back into line by colleagues – opponents, even – who felt that things were going too far too fast. At the end of 1987, he had been forced to acquiesce in the sacking of one of his most outspoken champions, Boris Yeltsin. His attacks at confidential Party meetings on the privileged personal lifestyle within the higher stratum of the Party (including, it is rumoured, Raisa Gorbacheva's) and his naming of individuals as being opposed to reform (including a high-ranking member of the Politburo, Yegor Ligachev) had finally gone too far for some people. Yeltsin's broom had swept too clean and he was forced to resign his post at the Moscow City party committee.

On the bright side, the official Politburo commission under Mikhail Solomentsev to rehabilitate the victims of Stalin was working steadily and by mid-August 1988 had publicly cleared 636 people who had been shot or sent to the labour camps. Among them was Nikolai Bukharin, one of the original group of senior Communists who started the October Revolution with Lenin. Bukharin had been arrested by Stalin and shot on a trumped-up charge of being a German agent. His rehabilitation was regarded as especially significant, because he had been a passionate advocate of economic reforms allowing some measure of private enterprise along the lines now suggested by Gorbachev.

Gorbachev initiated the withdrawal of Soviet troops from Afghanistan. The war was a humiliating defeat for the USSR.

From 1 January 1988 a new law had allowed individuals to apply to set up small businesses, and although there were complaints of excessive delays in the processing of individual applications, a trickle of entrepreneurs succeeded in getting their enterprises off the ground.

But bigger threats were posed to Gorbachev's policy of glasnost and democratisation: the economy was still faltering and no speedy solution was available to correct decades of mismanagement; the national minorities were restless particularly in the Baltic republics and a region of Azerbaijan called Nagorny Karabakh and there were ominous rumblings in the Eastern European countries like Poland.

The national minorities in the Soviet Union (about half of the total population) are largely a legacy of Tsarist times when over centuries of expansion neighbouring territories were annexed to Russia. The last additions to Soviet territory took place as recently as 1940 when Stalin took over the three Baltic states of Latvia, Estonia and Lithuania as part of a deal with Hitler in 1939. One of the sources of discontent in the Soviet empire is a gradual process of russification*, whereby distinctive national characteristics and language are subtly downgraded in favour of Russian. Russians hold many top jobs and the big decisions are mostly taken in Moscow. The first explosive situation erupted in Nagorny Karabakh, a small ethnic Armenian (and therefore Christian) enclave in the Muslim state of Azerbaijan. Local Christian Armenians felt that they had no political or economic power in their local affairs – all the power was in the hands of Azerbaijanis. Despite firm orders from Moscow

Perestroika, unlike glasnost, did not catch on. Queues remained long and goods in short supply.▶

to fall in line, the local government in Armenia remained sympathetic to the aspirations of the 160,000 ethnic Armenians to have more say in their own affairs in Nagorny Karabakh, and demonstrations continued to disrupt normal life in Erevan, the capital city of Armenia, throughout 1988. The situation had deteriorated so much by January 1989 that direct rule from Moscow was imposed.

Many Baltic States believed that Gorbachev's proposed new version of the Soviet Constitution would erode any claim for their right of independence. Previously, they were, in theory at least, voluntary members of the Union, whereas under the proposed new Constitution they would be permanently committed. In defiance, in 1988 the parliament in Estonia voted to assert their right to overrule legislation from Moscow. A compromise was eventually reached and amendments made to the Constitution.

As for perestroika and the economy, the *Guardian* newspaper's Moscow correspondent, Martin Walker, wrote in his farewell piece when he left the Soviet Union in July 1988: 'There is a grotesque and growing imbalance between perestroika in intellectual and political life and its almost complete failure in the economy. Unless very quickly they take the plunge and the political risk of ending the food subsidies, floating the rouble and opening the wholesale and retail distributive trades to private enterprise, I fear that the economic reforms could trickle away in the sands of the world's largest, most stubborn and most survival-conscious bureaucracy. Gorbachev cannot forever blame everything on the Brezhnev regime.'

The first sign of significant organised resistance to Gorbachev's reforms came in the form of a page-long article in the daily newspaper *Sovyetskaya Rossiya*, based on a letter written by a Leningrad lecturer, Nina Andreyeva. It was suspected that it was actually published on the orders of a much more powerful source, Gorbachev's main rival on the Politburo, Yegor Ligachev. The article was published in March 1988 while Gorbachev was in Yugoslavia, and aimed some telling criticism at the Gorbachev philosophy, accusing it of being 'left-liberal intellectual socialism'. The article was also reprinted on Ligachev's instructions and widely distributed with his recommendation that it be discussed in political education sessions.

It was clear that war of a sort had been declared. Gorbachev waited on his return until he had assessed the damage and support for the Ligachev attack, then retaliated with an article in *Pravda*, not published under his name but clearly recognisable by students of his style as his own work. The result of this confrontation was an uneasy truce. The Ligachev faction was unrepentant and the Gorbachevites were alerted to the potentially fatal opposition to their hopes of reconstruction and democracy.

The Soviet Communist Party conference in June 1988 published six resolutions, which included the right of public access to full and accurate information on any question except state or military secrets, including the promise of new legislation to protect freedom of debate. The other resolutions dealt with perestroika and economic reform, the reform of the political structure, the war on bureaucracy, inter-ethnic relations and legal reform. The reform of the Soviet legal system is one of the most thorny issues from a political point of view, since the concept of an independent legal system separate from the ruling party will involve a great political U-turn by the

Gorbachev faced strong opposition at the Party conference in June 1988, but unanimous voting at the top was still the 'norm'.

Party. Up to now, it has claimed to embody the law through the will of the people. This claim had never been put to the test of a free election. However, it was now announced that elections would be held for the first time in March 1989 with competing candidates not necess-

arily chosen by the Party for a new Congress of People's Deputies which in turn would elect a smaller regularly-sitting parliament. 'Democratizatsiya' – democratisation was firmly on the agenda.

Meanwhile, how far were perestroika and glasnost

The INF treaty being signed by Mikhail Gorbachev and Ronald Reagan in 1987.

changing the lives of ordinary Soviet citizens? And how did the new policies affect the world outside the Soviet Union? Some surprising things happened both at home and abroad in 1988 and 1989, and things would never seem quite the same again.

7
GLASNOST – AN INTERIM REPORT

In December 1988, Mikhail Gorbachev set out from Moscow on a historic trip. His itinerary was scheduled to be New York, Cuba, London. In New York, on 7 December, he addressed the 43rd United Nations General Assembly and announced that the Soviet Union was going to make extensive cuts in its armed forces. This was seen by many people as heralding the end of the so-called 'Cold War' between East and West. The 'Cold War' between the Soviet Union and its allies, and the USA and the countries of Western Europe had lasted since shortly after the end of World War II in 1945. A 'Cold War' is a war of propaganda, not of open military conflict. Fear and suspicion had bedevilled relations between East and West, resulting in a spiralling race to invent bigger and better armaments on each side. However, an INF (Intermediate Nuclear Forces) treaty had already been signed by the US and the Soviet Union in 1987, in which they agreed to destroy a whole class of nuclear weapons: all land-based missiles with a range of between 500–5500 kilometres. These included the Cruise and SS22 rockets which could have reached the Soviet Union from Europe, and vice versa.

In his 1988 speech to the United Nations, Mr Gorbachev said the Soviet Union was going to reduce the Soviet army by 500,000 men within two years. Also, 10,000 tanks would be removed from the countries of

Eastern Europe, as well as 8500 artillery systems and 800 combat aircraft. The new watchword was to be: 'reasonable defence sufficiency', in other words enough forces to safeguard the security of the Soviet Union, and no more.

As part of the total manpower cutbacks, Gorbachev announced a reduction in the Soviet forces (200,000) manning the eastern border of the Soviet Union with China and neighbouring states. He made it clear that these reductions would enable him to devote more of the Soviet Union's energy and resources to producing goods for the welfare of the Soviet people. In his speech, he even mentioned the possibility of converting armaments factories into centres of civilian production.

He went on to call for an acceptance by all countries of a variety of social systems. Previous Soviet policy had been to regard Communism as the only acceptable social and economic system. 'This new phase requires de-ideologising relations between states,' he said. Then he turned to the policy of perestroika and how it was progressing. 'We have initiated a radical economic reform. We have gained experience. At the start of next year [1989] the entire national economy will be redirected to new forms and new methods of operation.'

Gorbachev acknowledged that there would be, and already had been, setbacks. 'But the guarantee that the overall process of perestroika will steadily move forward and gain strength lies in a profound democratic reform of the entire system of power and administration,' he said.

This 'democratic reform' had two main cutting edges: the reform of the Soviet legal system, intended to provide the Soviet citizen with some independent guarantee of justice for the first time, and the new parliament to be elected by the (also new) Congress of People's Deputies. These were to be the first steps towards giving the Soviet citizen an elected representative voice in the nation's government. Fifteen hundred members of the new Congress were to be elected by the general public and 750 were to be chosen by the Party and 'public organisations' such as Unions and academic institutes largely controlled by the Party. These 2250 Congress members would meet only twice a year, their main function being to elect, in turn, a 452-strong Supreme Soviet or parliament sitting throughout the year to debate issues and pass new laws. The Congress would approve these new laws during its twice-yearly sessions. Elections were also to be held later in 1989 for local and regional government.

Gorbachev also promised in his speech that the Soviet Union would support the 'Helsinki process', a more or less continuous attempt by 35 countries to agree on ways to co-operate and achieve security in Europe. (This process is also known by the initials 'CSCE', standing for 'Conference on Security and Co-operation in Europe'). True to his word, an agreement was reached in January 1989 in Vienna at the third review of the whole 'Helsinki process' (so called because the first results were achieved in Helsinki in 1975, after nearly twenty-one years of frustrating post-war negotiation). The Vienna meeting produced a mandate for 'Conventional Stability Talks' between 23 countries aimed at achieving a balance between the non-nuclear forces of both the Eastern and Western blocs from the Atlantic to the Urals. Also a final document was signed with more specific pledges on human rights than had been agreed in Helsinki in 1975 and on the establishment of a more effective regime for checking that promises would be kept. This enabled the USA, UK and other countries of Western Europe to moderate their previous refusal to commit themselves to taking part in Gorbachev's proposed International Conference on Human Rights in Moscow, scheduled to be held in 1991.

But the optimism engendered by Gorbachev's speech at the UN was, sadly, short-lived. Both he and Raisa were

In the run-up to the election for the new Congress of People's Deputies, Soviet scientists protested against the exclusion of their candidates from election lists.

already looking grim and worried in the television pictures soon afterwards and later the tragic news was broken to the world: a disastrous earthquake had struck the southern Soviet republic of Armenia. Thousands were dead or missing. Whole towns and villages had virtually disappeared. An emergency of world proportions was declared.

The Gorbachevs made arrangements immediately to fly home from the USA cancelling plans to visit Cuba and Britain. In the new atmosphere of international trust and co-operation, offers of help from all over the world came flooding in. Over the next few days and weeks, a total of over 2000 specialist helpers from 70 countries were involved in the terrible task of digging for survivors amidst the rubble.

Two large towns in Armenia, Spitak and Leninakan suffered particularly. Shoddy construction methods had resulted in many modern tower blocks disintegrating when the quake struck. As the days after the tragedy dragged by, there was criticism of the role of some of the Soviet troops in the disaster area: young soldiers appeared to be doing little while exhausted local civilian rescue workers scrabbled with their bare hands at the ruins. The aid flooding in threatened to overwhelm the capacity of the local airport controllers. Two aircraft crashed while attempting to land supplies. The death toll rose gradually to an estimated 25,000, as hope was abandoned of finding survivors amidst the devastation.

The emergency threw up blunt comments in the Soviet media concerning the state of local and regional hospitals throughout the Soviet Union. Many lacked even the most elementary sanitation facilities, such as indoor toilets or running water. Disposable needles, plasma filters and other equipment needed to treat the survivors, were all in short supply. However, for the first time in Soviet history, offers of help from the international community were welcomed. Previously, such offers would have been refused. This time aid was welcomed and it flooded in. A total of £3 million in cash and £3 million-worth of goods was given by the British public, apart from the £5 million aid donated by the British government. Many more

The Armenian earthquake destroyed cities and killed 25,000 people.

millions were donated by well-wishers worldwide including £6.6 million from the European Community. This evidence of goodwill from the outside world had profound political significance, since for many years the Soviet people had been led to believe that they were threatened by enemies abroad. The friendly response of the West to Armenia's plight enabled the supporters of perestroika to argue successfully for greater arms cuts with the Soviet military. For the first time in many years, distinguished Soviet émigré musicians such as the famous cellist Mstislav Rostropovich and ballet dancers such as Mikhail Baryshnikov shared the stage with Soviet colleagues in order to raise money for the stricken region. The three Western allies (France, USA and Britain) responsible for West Berlin, part of the old capital of Germany which was divided after World War II, set a precedent by allowing a Soviet aircraft to land in their half of the city to collect supplies for the Armenian earthquake survivors. The outcome of the natural disaster was to strengthen the impression that glasnost really had changed the face of Soviet policy towards the outside world. Internally, though, more than 200 Armenian nationalists were arrested, including five members of the 11-strong Karabakh committee who had attempted to gain control of the rescue operation in place of the local Communist organisation.

It was typical of the progress of glasnost, that for every few steps forward there was the occasional step back. Steps forward included a real loosening up on permission to travel, for those who had friends or relations abroad. A step back was an attack in *Pravda* in January 1989 accusing Vitaly Korotich, editor of the campaigning magazine *Ogonyok* of a 'precisely formulated goal: to humiliate, to slander, to discredit'. But the world-famous prima ballerina Natalia Makarova returned to her native Leningrad to dance with the Kirov ballet company from which she had defected in London 19 years before. Also, the Western media were given unprecedented freedom to film aspects of Soviet life, such as a police investigation and the inside of a Soviet mental hospital.

Abroad, Gorbachev's policies had reaped enormous

benefits. Soviet troops pulled out of Afghanistan to the timetable previously announced, leaving the way clear for the establishment of a government independent of Soviet influence. The war had cost many soldiers' lives, but also an estimated million civilian casualties. More were feared in the struggle thought likely to ensue once Soviet troops had completed their withdrawal in February 1989. Gorbachev could justly claim to have instigated the end of the 'Cold War', and had achieved great progress in nuclear and conventional arms control. He had also indicated that for the first time the Soviet Union was willing seriously to discuss chemical weapons control. Governments and people in the West felt a genuine sympathy and support for his policies.

But the progress of perestroika at home, for which glasnost had been brought into play, was less of a success story. In theory, new methods of accounting for profit and quality control had been introduced. In fact, goods were in short – if not shorter – supply, and just as shoddy. Food was rationed in many parts of Russia in the winter of 1988/9. Due to continuing inefficiency, the harvest was dismal – many millions of tons short of the target. People complained that glasnost was all very well and good for the intelligentsia but it did not put meat on their plates or provide them with washing machines. Observers forecast the outcome of Gorbachev's policies as a race between the long-awaited material rewards promised by perestroika and the anger of a people who had gained nothing from his reforms except the knowledge of past misdeeds by the very party which continued to rule them.

'Dual control' at the top of some Soviet enterprises was an unresolved problem of the Soviet economy. Final executive decisions are hard to obtain when there is a political chief (an 'apparatchik' from the Communist Party) and a manager sharing power at the top. Also, the central ministries and the local party organisations both sought control over enterprises, but it was Gorbachev's aim to make Soviet industry independent and profitable.

People expressed strong feelings about 'Kremlyovka'. This is the slang Russian term for the privileges enjoyed at various levels by the Party. The lowest grade entitles the lucky recipient to free medical treatment at Party hospitals and to special food supplies. The highest grade permits unrestricted access to anything money can buy. There was pessimism about the willingness of the Party to give up these 'perks' voluntarily.

On the bright side, by early 1989 prospects for mutual understanding and peace had never looked better. The Soviet Union was inundated with applications to visit from Western tourists, all curious to experience glasnost on its home ground, and to accommodate them, many new hotels were being built (some as joint ventures with foreign firms). An agreement was signed to allow exchanges between 1000 Soviet and British schoolchildren over the next three years. Meanwhile the Soviet and American armies had begun destroying their stockpiles of unwanted nuclear weapons. Many other plans had been made for co-operation between governments and between individual organisations acting on their own initiative, with exchanges of art exhibitions, orchestras and theatre companies.

In March 1989 the elections for the Congress of People's Deputies were duly held. Many senior members of the Communist Party, including such notables as the mayors of Moscow and Kiev, the Leningrad Party boss and the Prime Minister of Lithuania, experienced for the first time the shock of losing an election. It should be added, however, that they showed no immediate signs of resigning their offices as a result. Boris Yeltsin, sacked for his outspoken criticism of Party perks, was triumphantly returned for a Moscow seat, having stated during his campaign that he thought political pluralism (allowing more than one party to exist) should be discussed. At its inaugural session, the new standing Supreme Soviet was elected.

As for the reform of the Soviet legal system: in February 1989 an independent association of Soviet advocates was set up in the face of strong opposition from the Ministry of Justice. This new association, supported by 2000 Soviet lawyers, aimed to improve the rights of the accused to a defense counsel, guarantee the independence of judges and establish equal rights – previously denied – for the defence and the prosecution. Up till now, the public prosecutors and judges have been controlled by the Party.

Within the Soviet Union, unrest continued in the republics. In April 1989, a flare-up between nationalist demonstrators and troops in Tbilisi, capital of Georgia, left at least twenty people dead. In June, 100 died in clashes between Uzbeks and Meskhetians (a Turkic minority 'removed' by Stalin from Georgia to Uzbekistan) and thousands were made homeless. In the economically ruined satellite countries of the Eastern bloc, the magnetic pull of a prosperous and increasingly united Western Europe exerted a powerful influence. Hungary and Czechoslovakia signed trade agreements with the European Community, and Poland was keen to follow suit. In the first real elections for 40 years, a non-Communist party, Solidarnosc, was to win almost every available seat in the Polish parliament. To counter this trend, Gorbachev launched a new theme calling for Pan–

In April 1989, Queen Elizabeth welcomed Gorbachev to Windsor Castle.

European co-operation under the catchy title of 'Our Common European Home'. Commentators observed that this appeal would carry more weight if the Berlin Wall*, symbol of European division since the 1960s, were removed as well as other barriers to free travel between East and West.

A flurry of diplomatic activity in Europe did pay dividends: at the end of a successful short visit to London in April 1989, Gorbachev invited The Queen to visit the Soviet Union and she accepted. Seventy years after her royal relations, Nicholas II and his family, had been shot by Communists, the time seemed ripe for the first ever visit of a reigning British monarch.

During many of the decades since the Revolution of 1917 it has only been possible to guess at what was going on in the USSR. Its fundamental secretiveness was summed up particularly well by Winston Churchill when he said that Russia 'is a riddle wrapped in a mystery inside an enigma'. As the end of the 20th century approaches, it is universally agreed that a change of an unprecedented kind is being attempted by Mikhail Gorbachev. It is to be hoped that his policy of glasnost will flourish because it seems to guarantee that the Soviet public and the world can never again be prevented from knowing the truth about the Soviet Union.

GLOSSARY

Anti-Semitism The practice of discrimination or physical violence directed against Jews. There is a continuing history of anti-Semitism in Russia, including regular 'pogroms' (violent attacks) in pre-Revolutionary times.

The Berlin Wall This wall was erected in 1961 when the Communist East German authorities attempted to halt the flow of East German citizens to West Berlin.

Central Committee A group of approximately 400 members of the Communist Party which elects the Politburo and oversees the work of the Ministries.

Collectivisation This policy was introduced during the Stalin era in the 1930s. It involved the confiscation of all farmland from the peasants and enforced pooling of their farms into enterprises belonging either to the State or the local commune. Up to 10 million people are estimated to have died as a result of the famine which followed the crushing of the kulaks.

Comecon The Council of Mutual Economic Aid, also known by its initials CMEA. A trading union with 10 full member states – Hungary, Rumania, Czechoslovakia, GDR (East Germany), Poland, Bulgaria, Vietnam, Mongolia, Cuba and the Soviet Union; four states with 'observer' status (ie they can attend meetings but are not full members): Yugoslavia, North Korea, Laos and Angola; 60 affiliated international organisations and three 'special observer' states: Finland, Iraq and Mexico.

Communism A political theory and system based on the philosophy of Karl Marx, which aims at a society founded on equality and communal ownership.

Fascism An extreme political movement which is nationalistic, authoritarian and undemocratic.

Feudalism A system of social rights and duties in 10th–12th century Europe, where land and protection was granted to vassals (workers) in return for services rendered to their lords, such as agricultural work or military service.

First Secretary This title was used by Nikita Khrushchev when he took office in 1953, to contrast with General Secretary Joseph Stalin.

Glasnost An old Russian word that has a common root with the Russian word for 'voice' (golos), which links it with the concept of voting (golosovat). Its old meaning is 'publicity' or a public announcement given at the end of a trial. Its new use is to describe 'openness' – part of Gorbachev's policy of restructuring the Soviet Union in a more democratic way.

KGB The Committee for State Security, in other words the secret police.

Kremlin The old fort in the centre of Moscow, formerly the seat of the Tsars of Russia and still used for government purposes. The word is often used to refer to the seat of Soviet government.

The Nobel Prizes These prizes for peace, physics, chemistry, physiology and medicine, literature, and economics are awarded annually by the Nobel Foundation. They were founded in 1901 by a Swedish multi-millionaire, Alfred Bernhard Nobel. The awards are highly regarded internationally, and winners receive a gold medal and citation as well as up to £25,000 prize money.

Perestroika The term used to describe Gorbachev's policy of reform in the Soviet Union. It means 'restructuring'.

Politburo The ruling body of the Communist Party and, therefore, of the Soviet Union. Elected by the Central Committee, it usually consists of twelve to fourteen full members, seven candidate members and eleven to twelve secretaries. The title of the leader of the Soviet government, 'General Secretary', arises from the tradition that the senior member of the Politburo holds the office of senior secretary of the secretarial group of the Politburo, although the secretaries are junior in rank to full members.

Reformation The great religious movement of 16th century Europe which attempted to reform the Roman Catholic church and led to the formation of the Protestant Christian churches.

Removal The practice of uprooting whole minorities from their homeland to another part of the country.

Russification The imposition of Russian influence through the insistence on use of the Russian language, employing Russians in certain key positions in industry and the government, and encouraging Russian immigration into an area. In other words, extending Russian cultural and political influence generally.

Upper Volta A country in west Africa, now called Burkina Faso. It is the poorest of all African countries.

Warsaw Pact A collective treaty of mutual military assistance to which the USSR, Poland, Czechoslovakia, the German Democratic Republic, Hungary and Rumania belong.

Young Communist League Youth movement for 14–26 year-olds which often leads to membership of the Communist Party itself.

FURTHER STUDY LIST

Reading

Moscow News (English language edition)
Soviet Weekly
Reports from the Soviet Union in the western quality newspapers.
Orwell, George, *Animal Farm* (Penguin Modern Classics, 1969)
The classic description of totalitarian takeover.
Solzhenitsyn, Alexander, *One Day in the Life of Ivan Denisovich* (Penguin Modern Classics, 1970)
Vladimov, Georgi, *Faithful Ruslan* (Jonathan Cape, 1979)
Tale of a gulag guard dog facing up to problems of readjustment when the camp is closed. A metaphor for de-Stalinisation.

Films

Agony (Elem Klimov, 1975)
Sympathetic portrayal of the last days of the Tsarist regime.
Come and See (Elem Klimov, 1985)
About the atrocities suffered by Russians during World War II.
The Commissar (Alexander Askoldov, 1967)
About the 1920s civil war in Russia.
Repentance (Tengiz Abuladze, 1984)
Deals with Stalin era in an imaginative way.

INDEX

The author and publisher would like to thank the following for permission to reproduce photographs:
Associated Press 88; John Massey Stewart 15, 20, 34; Novosti Press Agency 4, 6–7, 17, 25, 27, 50–51, 54–55, 59, 63, 74–75, 83; Popperfoto cover 29, 40, 43, 57, 68; Elizabeth Roberts 60–61; Society for Cultural Relations with the USSR 23, 76; TASS 80–81; Topham Picture Library 32, 39, 46–47; ZEFA 70–71